HAL•LEONARD INSTRUMENTAL PLAY-ALONG

VIOLA

Christmas SONGS

CONTENTS

To access audio visit:
www.halleonard.com/mylibrary

Enter Code
1365-2932-0601-6632

Audio Arrangements by Peter Deneff

ISBN 978-1-4950-2560-0

HAL•LEONARD® CORPORATION

7777 W. BLUEMOUND RD. P.O. BOX 13819 MILWAUKEE, WI 53213

Visit Hal Leonard Online at
www.halleonard.com

ALL I WANT FOR CHRISTMAS IS YOU

VIOLA

Words and Music by MARIAH CAREY
and WALTER AFANASIEFF

THE CHRISTMAS WALTZ

VIOLA

Words by SAMMY CAHN
Music by JULE STYNE

HAPPY HOLIDAY

from the Motion Picture Irving Berlin's HOLIDAY INN

VIOLA

Words and Music by
IRVING BERLIN

I WONDER AS I WANDER

VIOLA

By JOHN JACOB NILES

I'LL BE HOME FOR CHRISTMAS

VIOLA

Words and Music by KIM GANNON
and WALTER KENT

LET IT SNOW! LET IT SNOW! LET IT SNOW!

VIOLA

Words by SAMMY CAHN
Music by JULE STYNE

MARY, DID YOU KNOW?

VIOLA

Words and Music by MARK LOWRY
and BUDDY GREENE

THE MOST WONDERFUL TIME OF THE YEAR

VIOLA

Words and Music by EDDIE POLA
and GEORGE WYLE

MY FAVORITE THINGS
from THE SOUND OF MUSIC

Lyrics by OSCAR HAMMERSTEIN II
Music by RICHARD RODGERS

Viola

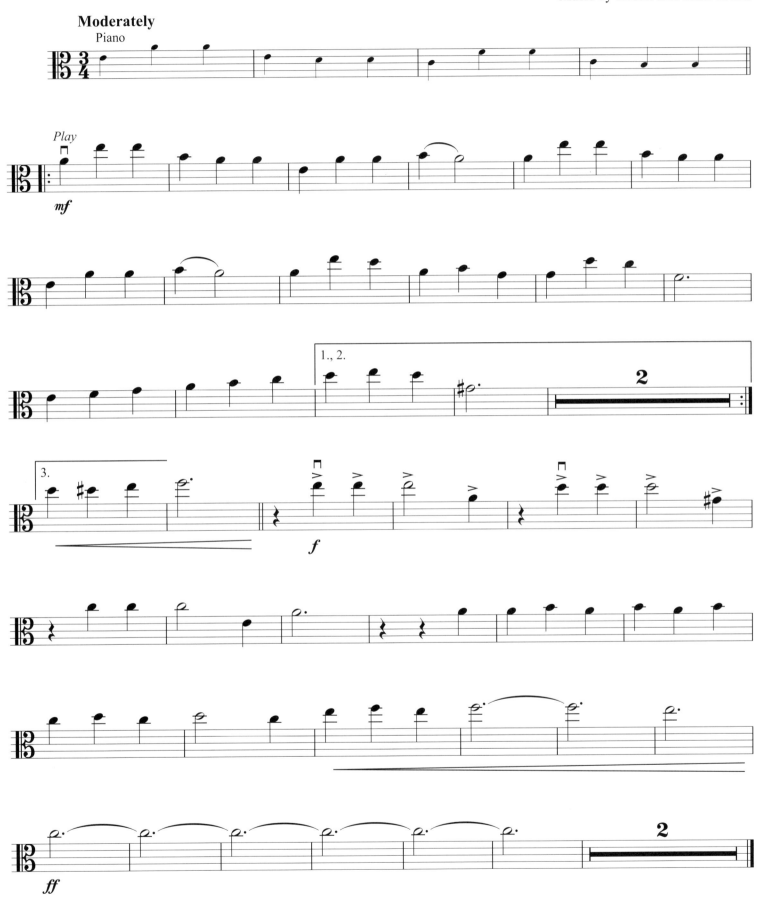

SILVER BELLS
from the Paramount Picture THE LEMON DROP KID

VIOLA

Words and Music by JAY LIVINGSTON
and RAY EVANS

THIS CHRISTMAS

VIOLA

Words and Music by DONNY HATHAWAY
and NADINE McKINNOR

WHITE CHRISTMAS

from the Motion Picture Irving Berlin's HOLIDAY INN

VIOLA

Words and Music by
IRVING BERLIN

HAL•LEONARD INSTRUMENTAL PLAY-ALONG

Your favorite songs are arranged just for solo instrumentalists with this outstanding series. Each book includes a great full-accompaniment play-along CD so you can sound just like a pro! Check out www.halleonard.com to see all the titles available.

Disney Greats

Arabian Nights • Hawaiian Roller Coaster Ride • It's a Small World • Look Through My Eyes • Yo Ho (A Pirate's Life for Me) • and more.

_____	00841934	Flute	$12.95
_____	00841935	Clarinet	$12.95
_____	00841936	Alto Sax	$12.95
_____	00841937	Tenor Sax	$12.95
_____	00841938	Trumpet	$12.95
_____	00841939	Horn	$12.95
_____	00841940	Trombone	$12.95
_____	00841941	Violin	$12.95
_____	00841942	Viola	$12.95
_____	00841943	Cello	$12.95
_____	00842078	Oboe	$12.95

Great Themes

Bella's Lullaby • Chariots of Fire • Get Smart • Hawaii Five-O Theme • I Love Lucy • The Odd Couple • Spanish Flea • and more.

_____	00842468	Flute	$12.99
_____	00842469	Clarinet	$12.99
_____	00842470	Alto Sax	$12.99
_____	00842471	Tenor Sax	$12.99
_____	00842472	Trumpet	$12.99
_____	00842473	Horn	$12.99
_____	00842474	Trombone	$12.99
_____	00842475	Violin	$12.99
_____	00842476	Viola	$12.99
_____	00842477	Cello	$12.99

Coldplay

Clocks • Every Teardrop Is a Waterfall • Fix You • In My Place • Lost! • Paradise • The Scientist • Speed of Sound • Trouble • Violet Hill • Viva La Vida • Yellow.

_____	00103337	Flute	$12.99
_____	00103338	Clarinet	$12.99
_____	00103339	Alto Sax	$12.99
_____	00103340	Tenor Sax	$12.99
_____	00103341	Trumpet	$12.99
_____	00103342	Horn	$12.99
_____	00103343	Trombone	$12.99
_____	00103344	Violin	$12.99
_____	00103345	Viola	$12.99
_____	00103346	Cello	$12.99

Popular Hits

Breakeven • Fireflies • Halo • Hey, Soul Sister • I Gotta Feeling • I'm Yours • Need You Now • Poker Face • Viva La Vida • You Belong with Me • and more.

_____	00842511	Flute	$12.99
_____	00842512	Clarinet	$12.99
_____	00842513	Alto Sax	$12.99
_____	00842514	Tenor Sax	$12.99
_____	00842515	Trumpet	$12.99
_____	00842516	Horn	$12.99
_____	00842517	Trombone	$12.99
_____	00842518	Violin	$12.99
_____	00842519	Viola	$12.99
_____	00842520	Cello	$12.99

Lennon & McCartney Favorites

All You Need Is Love • A Hard Day's Night • Here, There and Everywhere • Hey Jude • Let It Be • Nowhere Man • Penny Lane • She Loves You • When I'm Sixty-Four • and more.

_____	00842600	Flute	$12.99
_____	00842601	Clarinet	$12.99
_____	00842602	Alto Sax	$12.99
_____	00842603	Tenor Sax	$12.99
_____	00842604	Trumpet	$12.99
_____	00842605	Horn	$12.99
_____	00842606	Trombone	$12.99
_____	00842607	Violin	$12.99
_____	00842608	Viola	$12.99
_____	00842609	Cello	$12.99

Women of Pop

Bad Romance • Jar of Hearts • Mean • My Life Would Suck Without You • Our Song • Rolling in the Deep • Single Ladies (Put a Ring on It) • Teenage Dream • and more.

_____	00842650	Flute	$12.99
_____	00842651	Clarinet	$12.99
_____	00842652	Alto Sax	$12.99
_____	00842653	Tenor Sax	$12.99
_____	00842654	Trumpet	$12.99
_____	00842655	Horn	$12.99
_____	00842656	Trombone	$12.99
_____	00842657	Violin	$12.99
_____	00842658	Viola	$12.99
_____	00842659	Cello	$12.99

Movie Music

And All That Jazz • Come What May • I Am a Man of Constant Sorrow • I Believe I Can Fly • I Walk the Line • Seasons of Love • Theme from *Spider Man* • and more.

_____	00842090	Clarinet	$10.95
_____	00842091	Alto Sax	$10.95
_____	00842092	Tenor Sax	$10.95
_____	00842094	Horn	$10.95
_____	00842095	Trombone	$10.95
_____	00842096	Violin	$10.95
_____	00842097	Viola	$10.95

TV Favorites

The Addams Family Theme • The Brady Bunch • Green Acres Theme • Happy Days • Johnny's Theme • Linus and Lucy • Theme from the Simpsons • and more.

_____	00842079	Flute	$10.95
_____	00842080	Clarinet	$10.95
_____	00842081	Alto Sax	$10.95
_____	00842082	Tenor Sax	$10.95
_____	00842083	Trumpet	$10.95
_____	00842084	Horn	$10.95
_____	00842085	Trombone	$10.95
_____	00842087	Viola	$10.95

Wicked

As Long As You're Mine • Dancing Through Life • Defying Gravity • For Good • I'm Not That Girl • Popular • The Wizard and I • and more.

_____	00842236	Flute	$11.95
_____	00842237	Clarinet	$11.95
_____	00842238	Alto Saxophone	$11.95
_____	00842239	Tenor Saxophone	$11.95
_____	00842240	Trumpet	$11.95
_____	00842241	Horn	$11.95
_____	00842242	Trombone	$11.95
_____	00842243	Violin	$11.95
_____	00842244	Viola	$11.95
_____	00842245	Cello	$11.95

FOR MORE INFORMATION, SEE YOUR LOCAL MUSIC DEALER, OR WRITE TO:

HAL•LEONARD® CORPORATION
7777 W. BLUEMOUND RD. P.O. BOX 13819 MILWAUKEE, WI 53213

0315